To: John,
Thanks for every
you have been a great
if there's anything I can
for you, never hesitate to
Journey To My Deliver

Journey To My Deliverance

Looking back, to see my purpose

by

Chris Tann

Bloomington, IN   Milton Keynes, UK

AuthorHouse™
1663 Liberty Drive, Suite 200
Bloomington, IN 47403
www.authorhouse.com
Phone: 1-800-839-8640

AuthorHouse™ UK Ltd.
500 Avebury Boulevard
Central Milton Keynes, MK9 2BE
www.authorhouse.co.uk
Phone: 08001974150

© *2006 Chris Tann. All rights reserved.*

No part of this book may be reproduced, stored in a retrieval system, or transmitted by any means without the written permission of the author.

First published by AuthorHouse 2/21/2006

ISBN: 1-4259-1162-5 (sc)

Printed in the United States of America
Bloomington, Indiana

This book is printed on acid-free paper.

Dedication

This book is dedicated to my mommy, Rosie Luvenia Lane-Tann (1952-1995). I dedicate this book to you, in promise that I would do exactly what you said. You last wrote to me, "put God first", and "take care of yourself."

Putting God first has made me understand that there is a purpose, for my life. One of which I thought had no meaning. I Love You! I Love You! I Love You!

To my dad, Robert Howard Tann. Never mistake my truth as anger, but understand with my truth comes healing and a desire to love (the right way).

You are still my dad, and no one can take that away from me. We may never know why things happened the way they did, but with every trial, there is a triumph for us all. I Love You.

Acknowledgments

In order for me to know who I am and how I got to where I am, I had to look back over my life. In order for my purpose to be filled, corrections were needed and made. There are people in my life that I will be indebted to, for the rest of my time. I would like to thank the following people for their love and support. You are already blessed.

Lisa Tann- You are my love. We've gone through the fire, and we've been through the flood. You are a woman, so you will remain strong. I Love You!

Jamal Powell- It is no mistake why God has placed you here. You knew what was best for you, and it made me see what was best for me. I Love You!

Davey Wright and Keith Swinton- You are my laughter. You both are the reason that it was love that kept me. I Love You!

Robert Matthews -Your faith blesses me and your prayers protect me. I love You!

Donna Washington- You believe in me. You honor me. You encourage me. You are "my friend." I Love You!

Donnessa Victor and Rev. Vannessa Perry - You saw it, when no one else envisioned it. You prayed for it, when no one believed it. I Love You!

Russell Walker I- It is your blessing, that blesses me. You uncovered what was hiding from the world. Because of that, people have been inspired and blessed. You are my big brother. "If I can help somebody, then my living is not in vain." Your living is not in vain. I Love You!

Rev. Reginald T. Jackson and the Saint Matthew AME Church- You are all what family is really about. You helped me grow, even when I didn't feel like it. I Love You!

Vella C. West- While under your care, you were the parent that taught me. Despite where I came from, you saw God's work already in place. (My tears now shed.) Your living is not in vain. I Love You!

Contents

Introduction		xi
Chapter One	In The Beginning	1
Chapter Two	The Transition	8
Chapter Three	Is this normal (Traits)	15
Chapter Four	Becoming The Wrong Kind Of Man	24
Chapter Five	Becoming The Right Kind Of Man	29
Chapter Six	Coming Or Going	33
Chapter Seven	One Cold December Morning	38
Chapter Eight	A Change Is Gonna Come	42
Chapter Nine	I Know It Took A Miracle	48

Introduction

This is the true story of my journey. A man who never knew who he was, what he'd become, or what he was capable of being. It took circumstances for me to wake up and realize, that a change had to be made to get rid of the corruption of my mind. It is my prayer and hope that someone will get an understanding of the mystery, talent, confusion, temporary defeat, and challenged life of this man.

I share my story that someone is enabled to break the curse of generational failures and destroy barriers that were erected in the past. One of our many mistakes is that we allow our past to dictate or determine what our future will be. The sole purpose of, is to understand that I took a journey into the past in order for others to know how much I needed to make a difference not only in my life, but in the lives of young men and women who are suffering through situations that I have overcome. In addition, I want to enlighten those who have never encountered these events and depart the knowledge needed to avoid having their lives fragmented from the will of God.

Understand that the end result of all of this was good as a result of knowing a God that has the last word. In no way is this book to gain pity or sorrow for the misfortunes of my life. I say this because the overall greatness to my story is that I found a Saviour and he's sweet, I know. Certain names have been protected because of my love and concern for them. Be assured that all characters mentioned have seen and understood the life of a child who grew up, became everything they taught him, and will make the much needed corrections in their own lives as well.

Chapter One

In The Beginning

"In the beginning God created the heavens and the earth..." Later he created me! One spring morning, May 9, 1973, in Ahoskie, North Carolina, I opened my eyes. I became the second child, (as I got older, I realized) to parents who were not prepared to be parents. My childhood years allowed me to see what a traditional life was all about. The husband, the wife, and the two kids. Although there was no picket fence, backyard, or two door garage, there was still a sense of family. I had front row seats of a working class family, with the support of extended family. Everything that I saw on television, was everything I was living. What joy to be able to go over Grandma's house and have Sunday dinner and to play with cousins whenever we traveled to visit relatives. How the south seemed to have it's own way when it came to hospitality and more of a closeness. Never did I imagined this is where my life would take it's turn. But we will get to that shortly. As much as I anticipated visiting the south (North Carolina) as a youth, I would never have guessed it to be a place I'd despise in my adult years. If I had known then what the turn would be, would I have changed it, or could I, as a child? Swinging on Grandmas' tire swing with my cousins, going fishing with my uncles, seeing the entire family on the second weekend of every August, and watching grandmother, aunts and uncles on my mother's side, sitting on the porch, laughing and telling jokes was a joyous childhood occasion. While we (the kids), ran around the big house, or played Mother/Father May I, Red Light Green Light, or the ultimate favorite Hide and Go Seek. These events are most memorable because I saw closeness, happiness, commitment, but most of all, love.

Well the summer was over, and it was time to head back north.

We never knew planes or trains existed. Sleeping through four hours of an eight hour drive was a bit exciting as well. It was time to get ready for another school year. Time for school shopping and getting the things we (my older sister Lisa and I) didn't want. Oh but it was still refreshing to see the stern parents putting there foot down by saying, "it's not what you want, it's what you need." School was great and friends we had in excess. I remember having a friend who had a sister, that were friends with both Lisa and I. I would consider that my first best friend. It was great. Even though we went to separate schools, we'd always meet after homework was done. In the park was where we first met. I knew we had to be best friends, because his name was also Chris. I don't remember his sister's name. I don't think it matters at this point. I felt it was Lisa's friend anyway. We had to be friends for about two years.

I was six years old and I attended a school by the name of Nassau elementary. Now I believe it is named after Dionne Warwick. I will never forget that school. That's where I had my first crush. I mean she was beautiful. My first grade teacher. Light skin (that's how I like them), long hair and if I'm not mistaken we were the same height. Yea right, at six years old. I don't know how good I was (academically), but I know I never had to stay after like Lisa. I kind of think she (my first grade teacher) liked me because she selected me to be in the school play. I was to play a soldier with five other kids in the school. I remember this so well. We used to practice every Tuesday after lunch. The day of the play, my mother showed me a love that I never experienced before. I was on stage and ready to do the part I had practiced for weeks. I mean I had my steps down packed. When I proceeded to take my steps, I had to face the audience and who did I see, "MOMMY!", as I yelled out. After that I didn't remember any of my steps. But the most important thing I realized is not that I was in a school play, but mommy was there. As any mother would, she hugged and kissed me after the play and said I was the best lil' soldier on that stage. Sometimes we don't realize that when parents tell their children they are proud of them, it's the children who are actually proud of their parents. I only regret that this is one of the few times I felt proud of either of my parents. My teacher was proud of me as well, as she kissed me on the cheek. I was madly in love!

Then months later it happened. The first lady I was in love with, broke up with me. One of the teachers came in the classroom, while Ms. Teacher was out, and announced that we (our class) will give a party for Ms. Teacher. Wow! A party. Not such a great occasion. Yes, she was getting married. How come she didn't tell me personally?

Was it me? Were my grades getting worse? I needed an answer. I never worked up the nerve to find out. I remember telling Lisa about it on the way home. How distraught I was. I didn't even meet Chris at the park. What made matters worse, months later we were having another party. A BABY SHOWER! How can I move on from this?

Stay with me and you will see how this somewhat affected my life; however, there was something in store to soon make me forget.

One day my dad came to pick up Lisa and me. This was very unusual, being that Dad only came to the school once before. That was to see the principle about the two girls that were bullying Lisa.

Dad didn't play those types of games. Hey, that was his lil' girl and no one messes with his lil' girl. Dad was a giant to me. I thought he had the greatest job in the world. I used to go with him and people were always needing him to fix things. Wow, my dad was important. Dad was a tall slender man, very light skinned, with red hair and grayish green eyes. He loved basketball and was always "hitting" the basketball courts. Dad was one out of five children, (one deceased).

Nonetheless, we were excited to see him, and I ran and jumped into his arms. Dad didn't look too happy that day at school and we weren't going to question the rare look of unhappiness. We just walked in silence. We proceeded to go the route we often took, but suddenly made a slight change in direction. To my amazement, my inside thought questioned, "Why were we at the East Orange police station?

Why was daddy arguing with one of the officers?" He did it with fierceness in his eyes and posture. As Lisa and I sat outside the office, we didn't say a word to each other, but observed every movement of everyone. Suddenly, Dad came out of the office like a whirlwind. On the way home, I saw Chris and asked Dad if we could go to the park. "Not today, Chris. I'm taking you and your sister over your grandmother's." This was becoming a bit out of the ordinary, but we were going to Grandmom's, so it couldn't be something serious.

Yet I didn't know we would be spending the night, a school night at that. Even through all the events that had taken place, I don't know why Lisa or I didn't questioned the whereabouts of our mother.

The next day we were taken to school by a cousin. At the end of the day, we walked home and did our homework until mom got home.

Then it was back to the normal routine at the park with Chris, his sis, and Lisa. Before night, it was home bound for everyone. A few months later we moved closer to where our school was located. I was going into the second grade. The move was okay, but it meant less time to spend with Chris, being he was now a distance away, but I would still see him once in a while. We remained at the same school and took a similar route home. My how the new apartment had a lot of memories. From the apt. getting robbed, getting a bottle thrown upside my head (mistakenly, I presumed), with blood gushing everywhere. I could still hear mothers' voice, before she got to the door. "Didn't I tell ya'll to stop coming back and forth in the house?"

To her surprise as she opened the door she noticed the skin on my head was half off. Well, not half off. Even though it felt like it. Oh what attention I got that day. It always seems that when Lisa and I were in situations like accidents, going to the dentist or doctor's, we'd always end up at McDonalds. It was a bitter/sweet situation.

There's one day in particular that will stick in my memory forever. One night we were to go grocery shopping. It was the first time I ever heard my mother and father argue. At that time, I didn't give the argument a second thought. In my later years, I understood the argument over grocery shopping wasn't really about food. It was so serious or maybe not, that a physical confrontation took place. As sis and I sat and watched on the orange colored sofa, I remembered Mommy gasping, "I can't breathe". Lisa began to cry as I just stood there with nothing to say or feel. It was something I had never seen before; therefore I didn't know how to feel. After Dad ran in the bathroom and got a cold wet rag, he began to hold Mother and rub the rag over her, until she was able to revive herself. When Mother came to, all I could here my father say was "I'm sorry", repeatedly.

Nothing was discussed with Lisa and I. We didn't know reasons for anything. What we did know, we never went food shopping that night, we had Chinese for dinner.

Sadly enough, the arguments became more frequent each day.

I didn't know what to think or what was going on. Until one day, my uncle, grandmother, aunt, and my dad (which of course is his side of the family) were talking. Never did I hear such bad language and disownment towards my mother. I found out the reason why we took that trip to the police station that few evenings ago. Come to find out, one of the officers and my mother were with each other. "With each other? What's so bad about that?" I thought. "Why would Dad be mad about Mommy being with a police officer." When I think back, did Mommy have a reason? Was Daddy with any of the nice ladies he knew? I'm sure the police officer was nice to mommy. Did grandma, auntie, and uncle know about the ladies Daddy may have known?

Would they have been mad at Daddy? I wanted to ask Daddy why was he really mad. As a child, I stayed where I was taught...in my place.

As the arguments became more intense, I felt that something was going to happen, but I didn't know whether it would be good or bad, nor did I have a concern, for I didn't really know what was going on. We continued to go to school and meet with Chris once in a while, but one school day will forever be ingrained in my memory. It was around twelve noon, and I was called to the office. My teacher said to me, "Good luck in all you do young man." Now what am I to make of that? I went to the principle's office and I opened the door. To my surprise there was mommy with Lisa. "Hey honey, we are leaving early today." I mean is this great or what? A half day! We left the school and in the car was my uncle, (my mother's brother, who moved north). We went to his house. He lived in the apt. building that was across the street from where we once lived. He was hugging and kissing Mommy. Why were they shedding so many tears? Before I could gain the nerve to ask, a taxi pulled up, and my mother said to get in. Mommy, Lisa, and I drove off. On the way to where we were going, Mommy said to the driver "Don't go anywhere near that place."

As I looked out the window, it was where Dad worked at the time (Rayco on Central Ave.). We approached Penn Station in Newark, NJ." Mommy" I questioned, "where are we"? We were heading to Newport News, Virginia, on the Amtrak. "We are going to live with your grandmother, in North Carolina." On this train ride there were a plethora of flashbacks of years spent with Mommy and Daddy strolling through my head. I wondered, will Daddy be soon coming? Who will check under my bunk bed when the big monster appeared that always came to visit me? Will I be able to tell him about the four quarters I may get again when the tooth fairy comes to get my tooth?

Who will put together the toys and play with my Tonka trucks with me? Who will put together the race-car track that I break every year? I often wondered did anyone else think of the critical challenges that a six year old faced? I didn't want to question it then. The tears in my mothers eyes, revealed that she had her own critical challenges.

We arrived in Newport News. I'm not for certain who met us there. My memory seems to have its way of not remembering that which is not of much importance. I do know in order to get to grandmother's, we had to take an hour and a half drive there.

Looking Back

As a child I knew......

That people had come and gone, although I didn't understand their reasons for not staying, I thought accountably for improper decisions made by adults was mine. I saw lack of faithfulness between my parents, one that should not be shared by husband and wife, as my fault.

What I know now.....

Not to take the fault or have men/women present opportunity for me to hate my youth. A mans' spiritual authority results in spiritual character. One who teaches by what he believes, also teaches his life. I must be an example of the Word, or else I could destroy that which needs to be built up.

I Timothy 4:12

"Let no man despise thy youth; but be thy examples of the believers, in word, in conversation, in charity, in spirit, in faith, in purity."

Chapter Two

The Transition

Living with Grandma, I thought, would be great. We saw our cousins every weekend and sometimes during the week. The same experiences from summer vacation was now an all year event.

From time to time, I could remember going to church, but it wasn't something that was talked about at home. I do remember my grandmother saying we were going to have Bible Study. We (sis, my cousin Kim, and me), just sat through hours of Grandmother reading the scriptures, but never explaining the meaning of what she read. I do remember after the bible study we (kids) would go on the front porch and "play" church. I was the preacher and my cousin and Lisa were the choir.

The schools were completely different. Why was I the only one fighting? Why was I getting in trouble for stealing a classmates afternoon ice cream money, that he forgot on his desk? He forgot!

How do you forget about ice cream money? Even though my mother or grandmother never spanked me, they did yell a bit. I don't recall ever being spanked as a child. To this day, why can my sister recall it? As years went on, we were moving up and moving out. We were in our own place. I began to see more of my uncles. Mommy was really enjoying her time with her brothers and her sister. My mother's sister was one whom I adored. Aunt Janet and Uncle James had two beautiful girls. Their family reminded me of the family I once had.

When the family didn't spend time at grandmothers, we all gathered at Aunt Janet and Uncle James. She would take me for rides in her shiny black Ford mustang, and for my birthday (later years), she painted a portrait of Whitney Houston for me. What an exceptional artist she is. Cooking out in the backyard and playing badminton is a memory I cherish most. My Uncle James sort of took me under his wing. I later realized why this was so. Not only was he my mothers' brother-in-law, he was my fathers' first cousin. Before you think of anything crazy, let me explain. Two sisters married two cousins. Now that we've gotten that out of the way, my daddy's first cousin was the one who showed me how to fish and shoot a rifle. He took time with me. Even though he had a family of his own, he never failed to supply whatever I needed.

As years passed, we moved to Cofield, NC (one road over, with many fields in between from my mothers' sister). I began to see less of my cousins and more of my uncles. One of my fondest memories is when my mommy bought me a little red second-hand bike and my grandmother bought me a miniature pin-ball machine that they got from one of their yard sale excursions. I guess they succeeded in their attempt to fill a void in my life because I couldn't have asked for anything more. Then to my surprise my mommy bought me a brown and black German Shepard puppy. He was the first thing I'd ever been responsible for. His name was Chipper. I mean he was a champ. Everyday when I came home from school, he would run and jump on me like he'd been waiting for me all day. This was something different for me. I felt needed for the first time in my life. I actually loved someone who showed me that he loved me too. It subsequently became clear to me that he didn't have to give me anything to keep me occupied and out the way. It was evident Chipper loved me because he knew I hated taking the toilet bucket to the outhouse, but he was there walking right beside me. He became my second best friend. I couldn't ride my bike in the streets and Chipper would be alongside me as I rode my bike on the dirt paths. We would sit at the train tracks and watch the trains go by. As a child in North Carolina, watching the trains go by was like watching the

Macy's Day Parade. One day I came from school, Calvin S. Brown elementary. I was really looking forward to coming home and seeing Chipper. He was always happy and cheerful as a little dog could be. As the school bus pulled up to my house, I looked on my front porch for Chipper, but he was not there. I thought, "oh well, he must be in the house, or in the backyard." It did seem a tad unusual since he was always there. I got off the bus and went into the yard calling him. No response! I went into the house and again no Chipper. "Chris, honey!" I went into the kitchen from where my mother was "fixin" dinner. "Mommy have you seen Chipper?" Mommy said with an expression I can still remember, "Chipper was run over by a car." For minutes I stood there with nothing to say or feel. I could remember saying to my mom, "Okay, so where is he?" Lisa fell out of a moving car before, and she's fine. So my thought was maybe he was unable to move and he needed time to heal. I don't know why he ran out in the street anyway, for he never did that before. To my astonishment mommy broke it to me gently. "Chipper has died and he's never coming back." Well you know what the rest of the evening was like for me. The little red bike and the pinball machine didn't matter to me at that point. I went to bed early and was saddened for many days. Later on down the line my grandmother brought a pony, but that was short lived. It almost kicked me in the face and it later died. The pony didn't really compare to my dog Chipper.

 Now, I was nine years old and the family received a visit from who I call my favorite auntie. She was my grandmother's sister. So actually, she would be my great aunt. Vella West, or as I called her Aunt Clarice, stood about 5'4, 100lbs, fair skinned, with fairly long black hair. I mean this was a woman that I knew possessed something that separated her from anyone I'd ever knew. I couldn't put my finger on it, but I knew it was something. It was a short weekend stay for her. She lived in Portsmouth, Va. She was married, one child, lived in a beautiful home, with a garage. She had a lake in the back of her yard and a car that I always considered a limousine. It was stylish and classy. I remember the license plate so well. It read VCWest. Wow, how cool was that? Before her departure at the end of the weekend she asked if I wanted to come and live with her. I don't know whether it was a major discussion or issue for my mother, but

I'm sure there was a discussion. I mean who would let someone just take there child? With my departure, I was a bit saddened to leave my mother and Lisa, and I really didn't understand why I wanted to go so hurriedly.

When I got there, I felt like Willis and Arnold Jackson of Different Strokes. For the first time in my life, I had my own room, even though it was pink all over. I couldn't have the blue room, because that's her son's, who was then serving in the armed forces.

But hey, I was happy. The inside of this house was gorgeous. I'd never seen carpet all over the house. My grandmother had throw-rugs scattered throughout her home, but this was different. They had this thing called central air and heating. Do you mean to tell me I don't have to go outside and chop wood and bring it in? Even though they had wood in their backyard ,you only used it when you wanted to feel the warmth of a fireplace. I never saw two bathrooms in one house! I had grown accustomed to using the outhouse. They had two living rooms. There was one you weren't allowed to go in. One was called the family room and the other was the living room. That living room was immaculate. White bear-skinned carpet, with these long draped red curtains, an organ that sat there as picturesque as could be. Boy, this was the life for me!

I didn't understand why this woman, who came from the same stock was so well off, and yet others (not all), seem to struggle.

Maybe she just lucked up on the right guy. Of course, I found out why.

You see, she sat down and talked to me about someone who gave her all of this. She said if it had not been for him, it would not be possible. Well of course I wanted to know who this was, so I could tell mommy about him. From that point we started to have daily conversations about this man. I became more and more interested. I told her I wanted to meet him. She said, "Well tell me what do you know about him so far ?" I responded in the childlike manner of a ten year old, "Well you said, He created the heavens and the earth, and He sent His son down to die on a cross for the world, even me."

That's the part that got me. HE DIED FOR ME! "I know that while I'm here He wants me to live in joy and happiness, and prosperity. Then one day he wants me to live with him, because there are people on the earth who are destroying it. For he went to prepare a place for me, where the joy and the peace that I encounter down here will be 100 times better in his heaven." Who wouldn't want that? So at ten years old, I asked the Lord to come in my heart and be my savior. I attended First Baptist Taylorsville Church, in Portsmouth, Va. This church was cool.

Now I've been to church before in North Carolina, but it was not the same. This church took me in and had me sing my first song.

"Jesus loves me"! I don't know how I really sounded then, but I know people were always asking me to sing. In that year, my auntie and uncle helped me grow as a young man should. My Uncle Lemuel, a tall dark-skinned man about six feet who had served in the armed forces, would take me to the barbershop on Saturday mornings.

Occasionally, Uncle Lenny would take me to Tower Mall and buy me the mattel matchbox cars. I was so fond of the many colors, shapes and sizes. One day I came home from school and there was a collection of cars he'd brought me. I was so excited. It made me realize that it wasn't a gift that kept me occupied and out the way.

I know this because he would sit in his recliner and watch me play.

The look on his face, to see me happy, made me happy.

After Christmas, birthdays, good report cards, allowances, I'd already accumulated an Atari, toy cars, a brand new charcoal gray huffy bike, clothes, and good friends. I learned respect, honesty, faithfulness, love and the true meaning of family. Never did I see them argue and we all were at church on Sundays. What was also new for me was being at church a few times during the week. I will admit, there were times when I was tired of being at church so much. With each day, I became involved in new and exciting lessons and experiences that I never knew existed. Even though I was showered with so many wonderful gifts, nothing tops the love of two wonderful God sent parents. Yes, parents. What makes them great people is they loved everyone, despite the circumstance people put themselves in. Why do I say that? Towards the end of the school year, the pastor of the church's son was called into the ministry and had a church in Trenton, NJ. My Auntie and Uncle knew my dad was up there and made it a point to contact him, in order that I may see him on our short visit. There's really not much to speak on the visit, for it was very short. It seemed as if I just met a man and family that I used to know, and didn't know how to feel towards anymore. I did get $20 out the deal. Then we were back off to Portsmouth.

The school year had ended, and I decided to go to North Carolina for the summer to spend time with my mother and sister.

By this time, mommy and sis were living in Winton, NC. I could not wait to share what I learned and all the wonderful things that happened for me. I was so excited about being at that church, that I immediately went to the vacation bible school in North Carolina.

Jesus Lord of Promises was the theme for that year. I ended up staying, and attended school in NC. What made me want to leave all that was good and come to what was just okay? It's simple. I loved my mommy and nothing could ever take the place of my love for her.

Looking Back

As a child......

I knew that life could be better. I may not have known how to make it that way, but I knew there had to be a way. Although I was not fully aware, I began to see what a family grounded in God was like. It was obvious that this was the kind of life I wanted to live, a life filled with a special kind of love. I didn't know why this love given to me.

What I know now.....

I now realize that in order to have this life of love, God has given me a law.

It wasn't materialistic items that were given to love me, it was knowing that God had commanded that we must love one another. Christ's love to us is an example of how we should show love to each other. No one's duty is more frequently urged upon us by God, than that of a mutual love.

Chris Tann

John 15:12

"This is my commandment, That ye love one another, as I have loved you."

Chapter Three

Is this normal (Traits)

Lisa and I had gone to Triple C Bible camp that year, as we often did, but during our early ages we didn't really grasp why we were there. I thought it was to keep us busy and out of the way. I started to see less and less of mommy. I didn't know why. She didn't work and welfare supported the family.

Because one of my uncle's (mothers brother) was living with us, Grandma had moved from the big house and moved in a house in Winton. My grandmother had seven children. Five boys (one set of twins) and two girls. Most of the family was pretty close together. One of my uncle's was in jail for rape. He wasn't coming out anytime soon.

My grandmother (youngest of Tulie, Edith, and Vella) was a woman who believed in working hard. After the death of her husband who was struck by a falling tree, she managed to raise her seven children single handedly. Could raising her children alone and not having any father figure be the reason for their individual directions? Direction that lead most of them on the same misguided road. Four of the five boys were in and out of prison. Uncle George, the youngest of the brothers, was the only one who stayed out of trouble. He had his own place, a white Ford Tempo (stick shift) that he let me drive from time to time. He was great to all his nieces and nephews and was the family clown. They often say we look alike. We disagree. He thinks he looks better. Uncle George was at the house every once in a while and took care of me with a gift at Christmas and a dollar or two on my birthday.

The uncle that lived with us was the total opposite of my Uncle George. Physically, all my uncles were athletic muscle magnets. No one dared to mess with one, because you couldn't mess with one without messing with them all. So basically, no one was ever messed with. However, for one uncle I often wonder if he encountered the same dilemma's of confusion that I faced, in his youth. What I'm about to say is emotional for me, and have never spoken of in full detail about it, until now. When I was twelve, my uncle was the teacher of what some little boys faced, my first sex education class. I can't remember exactly how it all really got started. I do remember he would come in my room night or day, and would have me perform oral sex on him. Not knowing how to feel, I thought that because my uncle loved me, he wouldn't do anything that would hurt me. There were times when he would perform oral sex on me. Painfully, one particular incident involved anal sex; he would insert my penis inside of him.

From that, I developed scars and soars and it was hard for me to urinate for weeks at a time. Never did he try to reverse and do the same to me. Thank God! The oral performance became consistent, at least two times a week. If mother was home, these occurrences would take place late at night. Every time he released his sperm into my mouth. This was vile to me and I would always run to spit it out. I was afraid to tell anyone what was going on. I didn't even know if it was a wrong or right thing to do. I just knew it was different.

One day I was home alone and we got a new VCR. This is how I learned about video pornography. I saw everything from gay, straight, and animal porn. To a twelve year old, this was interesting.

My sexual curiosity was reaching it's peak. I wanted to try everything, except animal porn. That was just gross. I became more interested in the affairs with my uncle. When I think back, I didn't know how sick and perverted it had been. My friends and I often talked about what I've heard was something all little boys experience: boy on boy sex.

Journey To My Deliverance

Funny, I've only heard it from gay guys. To make things worse, on my thirteenth birthday, I was spending the night at my grandmothers. I believe the only reason why I stayed was because my uncle had moved out of our house and moved with my grandmother. I stayed in the room with him the night before my birthday. There were two beds in there. I slept in one, he in the other. That morning, he was doing something, that I've never seen (in person that is), and it became fascinating to me. He was masturbating. He did this as he looked at me. My curiosity, once again, was peeked. I began doing the same thing and after a few motions, the scariest thing happened. There was stuff coming from my penis and I felt funny but good at the same time.

Once I got used to it, it became habitual.

Time moved on and I saw less and less of my uncle. Either he was in jail or he had a girlfriend. There were times when I despised her for being with him or he being with her. As I became older, I began to experience more and more sexual encounters with boys and girls; next door neighbors, kids at school, and even cousins from both sides of the family. There wasn't much of a conversation about it. It (sex) was something we just did, playfully. I remember when friends and a cousin of mine had a club house. We would play what most kids play- "house". My cousin (female) always wanted to be the daddy. Out of five or six of us, no one questioned why she wanted to be the daddy. She would often "mess" around with another girl, so I assumed this was a normal thing. Most of my teen years I spent believing it was okay to have sex with both men and women.

Where was mommy you ask and what was grandmother doing? Well your guess on where mommy was is as good as mine.

More and more, mommy would not even come home and I would not sleep until she came through the door. There were times when I even thought she may have been dead. Even though I cried many nights, when she'd come through the door, I would hug and kiss her, and tell her how much I loved her. Even though she knew this, it never stopped. (One trait I picked up from mommy, that has been a mistake in my life, is that you know you do things wrongfully to others that love you, but you still take advantage of their love.) Oh how I wished I'd learned earlier! I would often ask mommy after days of being gone, where was she. With no emotion (another trait), I'd get a response such as, "I went to Bush Gardens" or "we went to the beach." I never knew why Lisa and I couldn't go and who was the "we", she was going with.

Well Lisa and I started to meet the "we(s)". So many I couldn't count (another trait). I would see acts that I saw on television. At that time the movie was the Godfather. Yes, a life of drugs, sex, money and violence. Instead of seeing breakfast, lunch and dinner on the table, there would be a powdered substance on one end and piles of money on the other. The cabinets were empty, but there would be piles of money on the table. I would go to friends' homes and steal food from their refrigerators. Sometimes, I would spend days at their homes, not for the company but because I was hungry.

I often spent more time at the home of the lady I called my Godmother. Ms. Sally Moore (deceased from breast cancer) invited me into her home. I felt that she loved me and would do anything for me. She was a teacher and had a love for children and was often bragging about her sorority (AKA). She lived in a big house, had the two bathrooms, and drove a Mercedes Benz. Even though I felt she had been in my corner, without telling her what I was going through, I began to steal food from her house. I believe I didn't want to tell her I was hungry, because I was afraid of what she would think of my mother. I didn't want to face the embarrassment. I would steal necklaces and earrings from my Godmother and present them as gifts to my mother. One particular incident, my Godmother came to the house, and my mother was sitting on the porch. I heard the horn blow and was eagerly ready to go. My Godmother decided to get out of the car and talk with my mother, as she so often did. On this occasion, my Godmother noticed the earrings that my mother was wearing and complimented her on them. My Godmother asked my mom where she'd gotten them, and of course my mom replied, "from Chris". As they say, a hush fell over the crowd. My Godmother asked me where I got them from, and I developed paralysis of the mouth. After a few sentences of going in circles, my mom and Godmother knew I had taken them from my Godmother's home. With a sadness and embarrassment on my mother's face, she apologized for me, and returned the earrings to my Godmother. I didn't go with my

Godmother that day and went back in my room. My mother later stated that she was disappointed, but understood why I did what I did.

That was more hurtful for her than punishing me. I wanted to show her that I could give her all she needed, and that she didn't need anything from the "we's". I wanted to show mommy that she didn't have to engage in the beatings and verbal abuse from them anymore.

I didn't want mommy to stab a man for calling her a bitch and almost watching him die in front of my eyes. Mommy later serve less than a month for that incident. Yes, less than a month! Hmmm!

I didn't see Grandmother as a way out. I became intimidated by her. When I would go over there, she would make me feel small by talking about the parents I was given. More and more I started not to stay at home (trait) and I began hanging out in the streets. Stealing and lying became easy for me. Now I was on my way to bigger things.

I was stealing out of local stores. Lisa was on her way with a baby.

Lisa and mommy decided to provide me this information as a gift. I never thought anything to present with such cruelty than a teenage girl in middle school, walking around pregnant, and I had to face the criticism of my peers. This had become an abandonment issue towards my sister (trait). What has happened that made me not once think back on the joy I had recently experienced in Virginia? No one was there to keep me on the track I should have been taking.

Was I responsible for myself as a teenager?

On top of this, confrontation between the "we's" and the family got out of control. Soon my Aunt Janet became a part of the lifestyle of drugs, adultery and who knows what else. I'm not here to say everyday was bad. For it wasn't, but the family that once sat on the front porch, laughing and joking no longer existed. Where have the family dinners gone? What happened? Please know, those weren't my thought's then. It was what I thought was normal. I've become accustomed (trait). Mommy wasn't in and out of jail, but the hospital always kept a bed for her. When the small town hospital couldn't adequately provide for her, she was off to re-hab. Remember, this was normal to me.

People never understand when they talk about Whitney Houston, someone whom I adore, the effect it has on me personally. I've seen addiction first hand. If we let the truth be told, I was becoming one too. Times when mommy was in the hospital, we would stay at Grandma's and it was one of the most horrific times in my life. I remember my grandmother gave me two dollars for my birthday, and said I could do anything I wanted with it. We went to this store (Roses), which was like the mall to us. Whitney had just released the single, "So Emotional". It was $1.49. I had to have it and

I did. When I showed my grandmother, she became enraged and scolded me. Grandma thought I should have brought a pair of socks or something I needed. Grandma said she would never give me anymore money, and I will learn my lesson when it comes to spending money, like I had it to throw away. Wasn't it my birthday money and she said I could do what I want with it?

Grandma definitely stuck by what she said. Grandma would get assistance when mommy was in re-hab and would buy Lisa things and I would never get anything. I remember one day when grandmother brought Lisa a teal winter coat and some pants. I stood in excitement awaiting my new clothes. To my disappointment, no clothes. Grandma would look at me and say, "Get that look off your face. You look like your father". Days later, from vacuuming my god-mother's floors and washing her car, she bought me a pair of jeans. I was happy to get these jeans. At that time everyone were bleaching their jeans. So you know me, I took my grandmothers' bleach from under the cabinet, and put my new jeans in her bathtub, and went to bleaching. I was done by the time she got home, but I think she smelled the bleach from her job. Before all hell broke loose, mommy was coming home soon. My mother took the vacant apartment right above my grandmother. Please notice how I didn't know Jesus, then I found him, then I forgot about him (trait).

Can I blame it on being young? Okay, let's move on.

Mommy is back and although she kicked the habit, she was never the same. It seemed all hope for life was gone, and she was on earth existing (trait). The woman who stood about 5'8 140lbs, now gained over 50lbs, since our move to North Carolina. No more did mommy have the medium length hair. She resorted to going with the very low cut. I wouldn't say mommy didn't care if I was coming or going, but she seemed to not have the energy to fight the issue. So I did whatever I wanted. Along with my "god-brothers", we started hanging out with "the crowd". We became infatuated with the idea we were hanging with people who had cars and jobs, and not the boring high school kids. Sex became different for me. It seemed passionate and yet more desirable each time (trait). These were friends that my god-brothers and I felt, had our back. We really didn't do anything out of the ordinary. We were in the deep woods of North Carolina. We would just ride around and, at the time, drinking or smoking wasn't really my thing. My god-brothers and I would often have sex with some of the girls and yes at times, the guys. I began to wake up thinking this is what was most important to my day. I would get up, get dressed and just go. Then one day something happened.

Strangely, mommy asked me where did I think I was going. Huh? I don't think I heard correctly. She repeated herself. She stated she's noticed the crowds I've been hanging with and that today I wasn't going anywhere. I thought this lady was really crazy. What made her think she could tell me what to do? I was grown. I am fifteen years old.

My friends pulled into the yard and with a look I've never seen before, mommy told them, "Chris will not be going anywhere with you, anymore". So you can get out of here!" Before I could say anything, they were gone. I became angry. I became more rebellious and I started becoming sneaky. Leaving in the middle of the night without telling anyone (trait). Well it caught up with me. My mother grounded me. I knew what grounding was from living in Va. But does this happen in NC? I couldn't take this. Something had to be done. From the seldom visits and calls from my father, I decided to give him a call.

What made me call my father and make up lies that I was being unfairly mistreated (trait)? He told me to go to one of his cousin's house, and ironically I had family from New Jersey who was coming to visit and I could ride back with them and stay with my father. This was great. I stayed at my cousins' house, where I lived more off snickers and water for a week. Snickers that I shared with mice that ran rapidly throughout the home. Finally they had arrived. With my mother not knowing where I was (I think), she finally got a called when I arrived in New Jersey.

Looking Back

As a child I knew.......

What ever was taught, is what I learned. I knew that what I saw loved ones' do, couldn't hurt me.

What I know now.........

That I was lured into sin. I know that I can not do the same as those who afflicted me. Sinners love the company of sin and they entice with flattery and speech.

Proverbs 1:10-19

[10] My son, if sinners entice thee, consent thou not. [11] If they say, Come with us, let us lay wait for blood, let us lurk privily for the innocent without cause:
[12] Let us swallow them up alive as the grave; and whole, as those that go down into the pit: [13] We shall find all precious substance, we shall fill our houses with spoil: [14] Cast in thy lot among us; let us all have one purse: [15]
My son, walk not thou in the way with them; refrain thy foot from their path:
[16] For their feet run to evil, and make haste to shed blood. [17] Surely in vain the net is spread in the sight of any bird. [18] And they lay wait for their own blood; they lurk privily for their own lives. [19] So are the ways of every one that is greedy of gain; which taketh away the life of the owners thereof.

James 4:7-8

"Submit yourselves therefore to God. Resist the devil, and he will flee from you.
Draw nigh to God, and he will draw nigh to you. Cleanse your hands, ye sinners; and purify your hearts, ye double minded."

Romans 6:12-18

Let not sin therefore reign in your mortal body, that ye should obey it in the lusts thereof. Neither yield ye your members as instruments of unrighteousness unto sin: but yield yourselves unto God, as those that are alive from the dead, and your members as instruments of righteousness unto God. For sin shall not have dominion over you: for ye are not under the law, but under grace. 15 What then? shall we sin, because we are not under the law, but under grace? God forbid. 16 Know ye not, that to whom ye yield yourselves servants to obey, his servants ye are to whom ye obey; whether of sin unto death, or of obedience unto righteousness? 17 But God be thanked, that ye were the servants of sin, but ye have obeyed from the heart that form of doctrine which was delivered you. 18 Being then made free from sin, ye became the servants of righteousness.

Chapter Four

Becoming the wrong kind of man (I know)

Mommy expressed her disappointment and was sadly hurt, but later agreed, maybe being in New Jersey was best for me.

New Jersey again. Not in anyway like Virginia or North Carolina. I adjusted pretty quickly. Daddy wasn't much different from mommy; before her aggression stage that is. I think Dad wanted to make me happy in anyway possible, so he refrained from doing anything that would make me resent him. Wrong move! So I ran wild in the Garden State. I had a friend next door that I hung with everyday. Whether it was sitting on the stoops at my grandmother's (my father's mother, of which I stayed), or sitting on my friend's stoop.

Sometimes we would skip school and stay in his house playing Nintendo's Super Mario Brothers, til it was dark. We became very close and he would often invite me to his church and I would go because of the things he would tell me. So I decided to go to Saint Paul Fire Baptizing Holiness Church, in Newark, NJ. They had another name for Saint Paul FBH, (but that I will leave that alone).

I started to like the church because all they really did was sing.

There was a "crowd" that I became attached to. I would often go even when my neighbor didn't go. I began to hang out with them outside the church. This to me was great. Who cared they were twice my age. I began to indulge with one particular lady who would buy me anything I wanted. Not only was she into being with men, she was well-liked by ladies. She introduced me to the gay and lesbian women that attended her church, and we would often meet at her home after service. It was definitely an environment that you wouldn't have even thought we were in church earlier that morning. There was drinking and weed smoking, along with conversations about everyone in the church. Not good conversations. I never took part in the conversations, only being, I really didn't know anyone in the church and wasn't mature enough to participate in a conversation on their level. I remember they often made comments and jokes about the older lady sleeping with me and how I was jail bait to her. Yet they never had a problem with approaching me in the same manner in which she did. I did resist. I was satisfied with just being with her. As long as I would see her and go to her church, she would shower me with anything I wanted. My thoughts became distorted. I thought back to when I was ten years old. I started going to church and was getting gifts. I figured hey, if I just go to church, I could get anything I want.

This couldn't hurt. It was once a week. Although they were in church practically all day, I could bear it. However, this is no comparison to when I was ten years old. A totally different kind of love, it was. She would often buy clothes for me, and I would always have money. She bought me the trench leather coat that everybody was wearing at the time. My father did question it, but my lies covered it. There it goes again. If I can get away with it and you still love me, then I took advantage (trait).

School was a bore for me. I had no intentions on learning. Since Dad or Grandmother rarely checked for report cards, I would skip most classes except English and chorus. I think dad had something to do with me passing English. He was very fond of my English teacher.

She was a fox. School for me were just days to sit in the building and think about what I will do when I got out or what I was doing for the weekend. You know what's the sad part. I passed with no problem.

Don't know how and I don't know who. Could it have been the young lady who lived across the street, that claimed me as her little brother?

She was the captain of the cheerleading team, and president of every organization imaginable. The teachers I had were in awe of her.

I saw much of Dad. He would come over every night when I was up here. He had a girlfriend that was much younger than him (trait), and wasn't fond of children. If I were to go on intuition, I would say Dad had more than just Lisa and I. My grandmother had a neighbor with kids, in which all three looked like or resembled my dad.

Let's leave that one alone! THAT'S JUST MY INTUITION!!!

That summer rolled along and Lisa came up to spend the summer. I was so excited to see her. Although Lisa didn't have the little one with her, due to a loss of custody to my grandmother, she was still in good spirits. I don't know if you could call it a custody win.

Lisa was still seeing her son everyday. Maybe you can call it a win.

Lisa had no say so in his life. I didn't see much of Lisa on her visit, being it was summer. I was doing things that were productive. I entered the Mr. Black Teen NJ Pageant and became the first runner-up. It is also where I got my first job. Roy Rogers. How I loved their biscuits. I would take some and go in the bathroom and just eat five or six at a time. When I had free time to spend with Lisa, we would play in the streets with other kids on the block. Oh how I remember that so well. Being that I was still new to New Jersey and she was, well still country, the kids would laugh when we would say, "Get out the road, car coming". They would quickly say "road. A road has dirt, this is a street." Boy how we look back and laugh.

The summer was coming close to an end. August came around, and I had to get the rest of my fun in before the summer was over. I wanted to go hang out one night, but my aunt took control of that situation and said it was too late for me to be going out.

Flashback, "She must be crazy." I was grown. I am sixteen years old and I have a job. Of course this is what I stated to her. My aunt informed me if I wanted to do what I wanted, then go live somewhere else, since I was grown. Being who I thought to be big and bad, my reply was, "I don't want to live in this hell hole anyway." The look in her eyes, as well as grandmother's, well let's say if looks could really kill. I don't know why they didn't retaliate. My aunt called my father and told him what happened. Well, yes well, just before I was going out, I was getting my shoes from the top of the stairs, my father came in raging. The last time I saw this look was at the police station, years ago. I didn't hear anything he said, all I remember is he hit me so hard, I fell from the top of the stairs, all the way to the bottom. This was it for me. The next day I had to plan and do something. I couldn't live with the lady who had showered me with all that I wanted. By this time what we had was wearing thin, and I no longer had a desire to be with her. I didn't want to go back to NC. Even though my lifestyle wasn't any better in New Jersey, I couldn't do NC again. The light bulb!!! Hey why don't I call my aunt in Va.? I asked if I could come for the rest of the summer, until I go back to school. I didn't inform my dad or anyone else where I was going. Being the smart woman my aunt (VA) is, she called my father before I got down there. Aunt Clarice received full details of what happened. Just when I thought I outsmarted everyone, someone is always smarter.

Looking Back

As a child I knew.....

That my way was the only way. No one could provide for me, but me. I did it when I wanted to and how I wanted to.

What I know now....

That my choices will create my future. My decisions will either bless me or curse me. In order for me to know the way of God, my soul can not become sick from making the wrong decisions.

Deuteronomy 30:19

"I call heaven and earth to record this day against you, that I have set before you life and death, blessing and cursing: therefore choose life, that both thou and thy seed may live"

Proverbs 3:5-7

[5] Trust in the LORD with all your heart, and do not rely on your own insight.
[6] In all your ways acknowledge him, and he will make straight your paths.
[7] Be not wise in your own eyes; fear the LORD, and turn away from evil.

Chapter Five

Becoming the right kind of man, (I think)

Back in Va. Oh what a relief! Or so I thought. Even though I felt a sense of comfort, it seemed as if something was bind before I entered the house. I stayed there, met up with my old elementary friend who lived down the street. He was the only one I was allowed to associate with, unless it was someone from church. I had this thing called curfew. "What is that?", I asked. She informed me that I had to be in the house by 10pm. What made this interesting was I had no problem with that. I enjoyed being there and in her presence. Aunt Clarice made it a point to meet my friend's family again, since it had been so many years. Auntie and I had many talks. Whether it was in the car or sitting in the kitchen as she prepared meals. She had a way of making conversations fun. I can recall her standing about 5'4, in the kitchen and I would say something, and she would say "Maaannnn are you crazy"? Her laugh behind that is a picture that will stay in my head forever. I felt comfortable in asking if I could finish my Junior and Senior year with her and Uncle Lemuel. After a discussion with Uncle, it was set. I was enrolled in high school, and because the credits in northern schools are slightly higher, it gave me the chance to take more electives. We all know electives are a breeze.

So here I am meeting new friends, and going to auntie's new church, Centennial Baptist. Being in at 10pm on weekdays, 11pm on weekends wasn't a problem for me. Now I'm in Sunday school and singing in the youth choir.

I'm dating a cheerleader who was the most beautiful high school girl I'd ever met. I mean she was fully loaded. My aunt would never let her come to the house. She would always say the man goes to the woman. So there I was, either walking or having my aunt drop me off. My girlfriend and I often had sexual encounters, and I found myself wanting more of her, everyday. At times I felt I wasn't enough for her, because she always had her ex-boyfriends around and she would often speak on how great they were in bed. I felt I was always in competition. One particular occasion where we just finished having sex, she ask me a question that made me insecure towards women for a short period of time. She asked me, if I ever did it with a guy. I was completely startled. I mean who asks that after you finish having sex? Of course, I denied it. For days I thought about why she ever asked me that. Our sexual encounters became less and less, and so you know what that meant for our relationship.

I started working at Leggett's department store. This was great for me. I was buying my own clothes. The Christmas of my junior year, I went to visit mommy and Lisa. They told me they had a gift for me. How excited I was. I bought them tons of Christmas gifts. We never had Christmas where we'd give gifts and have a festive tree. I knew this Christmas was going to be special. I remember during my pre-teen years I would get a tree out of the woods and get lights from God-mother and decorate the tree. I would wrap items that were in the house, and put mommy and Lisa's names on them. Even though my friends were getting bikes, toys, shoes and clothes, I was content just being with mommy and Lisa, and looking at the tree that I decorated. How happy I was to see them. Mommy and Lisa still lived above grandmother. The first thing I did was hug and kiss them.

Mommy asked if I wanted my gift now. You don't have to ask me twice. With Lisa's smile wide as an ocean, mommy said "you're going to be an uncle again." I refrained from showing the disappointment on my face, and I smiled on the outside, while I broke down on the

Journey To My Deliverance

inside. At this point I didn't want to do the gift exchanging ever again in life. My thoughts on the entire winter vacation were merely that my sister was having another baby at 17, and now a junior in high school like me. I returned back to Virginia and proceeded to finish my junior term.

Now it is senior year, a club officer, still working at Leggets, and no longer with the cheerleader. The passing of my uncle took a major toll on my life. This was a man who bought me toys and watched me play as a child. Aunt Clarice showed me that she was the ultimate strong black woman. Auntie stuck by Uncle Lemuel's bedside til the very end. Shortly after that, my mother's brother was run over and killed in a tragic car accident. Not the one who molested me, even though sometimes....well never mind. Senior year came to an end. I graduated with no where to go. One thing I don't understand, is that it was never a question of what my future would be, even with auntie.

For the most part, I think it may have been a financial issue. After several attempts to get into a design school in Miami, money was always a problem. Our last breakfast together, I sat across from Auntie and mommy sat in the middle. I never cried so much over fond memories that auntie and I shared. To this day, she reminds me of the first birthday party she ever had, that I gave her. "I will never forget it, I was so surprised. It was one of the best days of my life", she adds. I sometimes wonder what ran through mommy's mind as auntie and I sat there crying and reminiscing. This was something we never shared as mother and son.

So here I am, on my way back to NC. I didn't know where I would lay my head. After two years I was so accustomed to living in the beautiful home on the lake. I couldn't force myself to go back to the roach infested home that my mother moved into. I don't understand why she decided to go back to Ahoskie. You wonder why I didn't stay in Va.? Trust me, there were many attempts of rooming with high school friends and continuing to work at Leggets. This of course was very unsuccessful. To stay with my aunt was out of the question. Well we have a traditional aunt who believes at 18 you are a grown man, and now you are your own responsibility. So I stayed with my cousin Kim in North Carolina until I found out what my next move would be. I didn't know what to do. I was completely lost. I was out there, going days without eating. My cousin didn't have much, but I wasn't sleeping on a bench or the ground. My dad came down to visit.

Light bulb? So the questioned arose, "Can I come up there and get a job?" This again saddened my mother. She was more worried about me being up there as an adult, than as a child. If I would have stayed in NC, I feel none of these pages would be readable.

Looking Back

As a child I knew....

I was actually sent to this place for a reason. I wasn't quite sure, but everything seemed to be falling into place. I started to feel at peace. I knew there were still some adversities, but they weren't for me to handle. I was still not considered an adult..

What I know now...

I am responsible for my life. No one can take care of Chris, but Chris. I will continue to face trials, but I will live in peace. Through whatever I may endure, I must remain joyous and prosperous.

John 16:33

I have said this to you, that in me you may have peace. In the world you have tribulation; but be of good cheer, I have overcome the world."

Chapter Six

Coming or Going?

New Jersey again. No job in site. Some friends are still around, but my contact with them was not important. I met a crowd. It wasn't hard to find. I could just walk out my door and would be suddenly approached. This crowd was people who I've never knew about.

They were different and often had me laughing. They included me in their circle. We would hang out at a club. First Choice was the name.

There were just a few women, but wall to wall men. I was getting attention that I never received before. Not having any money, I would always have something to wear, admission to the club, and drinks unlimited. I started hanging out and not coming home (trait). This crowd became my family. They showed me attention and gave me what I thought was love. Never did I imagine there were ulterior motives behind it. This crowd was truly different than any crowd I'd ever experienced. To them, I was new territory to conquer, use and destroy. After the accomplished mission, I was tossed to the side and was no longer of the crowd. I started doing what they did. I became accustomed (trait). My mission was to conquer, use and destroy. Anyway I could manipulate you to get you in bed, I would do just that. Once I had enough of you, it was time to move on. Whether you liked it or not, you knew not to cross me. I was a fighter and I would fight you at the drop of a dime. I didn't care about anyone's feelings, or how much I hurt them. I never took the time to give thought to whether this was right or wrong. I just knew it was something that was being done. Somehow it became boring to me. It was getting old. The people became old and the new weren't offering much more of anything I hadn't had before. I had to move on. They (crowd) started to have what is commonly known in the gay scene as balls. This was something I knew wasn't for me. Let me be very clear, not everyone who leads a gay lifestyle is wrapped up in to many of the "scenes".

Staying at my grandmother's, life was becoming harder everyday. I decided to enroll in a two-year college. While trying to obtain financial aide, I looked behind me in line, and there was a guy, whom seemed to be watching me. I later avoided him and went home. Hours later, the phone rang. It was him. I asked Reggie how he obtained my number, and Reggie stated that he saw the number on my application. I was honestly impressed. We began to hang out and became the best of friends. He was about ten years older than I was. I began to learn a lot from him. What I never knew about being independent, I learned from Reggie. My time was centered around him. There wasn't a day I didn't want to be without him. We moved in together and I started working part-time. I was still seeing girls but became less interested as time progressed. Reggie introduced me to his friends. I had Christmas's that I had when I was in school, but better. A beautiful apt. in New Jersey and in Atlanta. The first years were smooth. Or so I thought, I began to uncover lies. I experienced unfaithfulness, deceit, and betrayal. Never had I encountered such fury. Yet, I still maintained my love and dedication. I did anything I was asked. How do I know I was in love? One day I walked from Orange to Irvington, just to see Reggie. He would often spend nights over his grandparents. I had no money. It took me about two hours to get there, in the freezing cold. I was treated any kind of way. Because I was in love (or thought I was), I kept doing whatever was wanted and my love was taken advantage of. Is this how it was supposed to be? It came to a point where I felt as if I couldn't and didn't take it anymore. I came home to abuse, and promiscuity. That, I felt was the end. I ended up cutting my wrist and taking pills-A method that

Journey To My Deliverance

my mother used in her several attempts to suicide. How silly was I? If that didn't work for her, why would it work for me? I ended up at East Orange Hospital. The psychiatry ward is where they put me. For days, I was put in a confined room with people who had really lost it. This was not me. Upon my release, I sat in the car with my father, who said the words to me, "I never want to see you like this ever again." Could that be all you have to say to me? I decided it was time to make changes. The love of my life went and decided to love two of my friends over again.

Two years after the relationship was over I was informed that Reggie was dying of HIV/aids. One thing I was smart about was my aunt telling me to practice safe sex. However, you can never be too sure. Tested immediately, I went through the worst three days of waiting, in my life. Prayerfully, I was called to say I was fine. I didn't go and get tested again until years after, being that I was scared of the doctor saying it could still show up down the line. After being tested years later, I again was blessed by his mercy. I moved on still in one female or male relationships after the next. I was in rare contact with my family, but spoke to my mother and auntie as much as I could.

By this time, after the suicide attempt, I had become a member of Saint Matthew AME Church. Out of all the churches in the Essex County area, God placed me where I needed to be. I developed a relationship with God and a somewhat steady prayer life. I wasn't as strong as I needed to be, but I saw myself moving into the right direction. I joined one of the five choirs. Immediately, I felt a sense of having a family. Saint Matthew was where I wanted to be 24hrs/365 days a year. I wanted to run or get away from all that I dealt with and was dealing with by going to Saint Matthew. Not realizing that Saint Matthew couldn't help me face and deal with all the pain and hell I was still creating for myself. I wanted to move away from the hell, so instead of dealing with everything I went through, I began putting on heirs. I made it seem as if I was always happy and this strong individual on the outside. I began to practice this routine so much, I started to convince myself that I was everything, but I really was not. It became so real to me, that I began putting on the heirs everywhere and to every person I was around. Yet, I still kept praying and reading the scriptures. I was living with so many different personalities, that it didn't matter who I was for the day. If I woke up and wanted to be nasty to whomever I was around, that's who I was. If I wanted to be the spiritual person for the day, that's who I was. I started to make moves. I met Davey, Carlos, Keith, along with a host of other friends.

Some who were genuine and others were just plain nugatory. Even though they didn't go to the same church, they were in church. These were the friends that, even to this day, let me know when I'm wrong, and applaud me when I'm right. I developed a strong love and care for them and felt they had my back no matter what. They weren't out to devour me or use me up. They believed that I was much more of a benefit to them, than they were to me. I had friends who were just friends.

Even though Carlos, Davey and Keith were around, I was still looking for an intimate love. One after another they became failures.

My fault on many. I was tired of giving my love and in return having it stomped on. Since no one ever cared, then why should I. Was I developing emotions and feelings? Did I already have them and didn't know what they were? I started dating for convenience. It was the more you do for me, the less I'd do for you. If you didn't do for me, you were tossed aside and or verbally abused for not caring for me like I wanted. Soon I noticed that people gay or straight were intimidated by just my presence alone. I took advantage of the opportunity. I was bold in everything I did. Realizing now, that I only took advantage of any situation because that was my strength and a way for people not to get close and see what was really going on inside. I started driving nice cars, that weren't mine. Living in houses that I didn't own. Wow, is this what they call exploring your 20's? I had not a care in the world. I didn't have to work. I was being taken care of by two or three people at a time, and didn't know I was selling my soul to the devil. My name was being engraved in the pit of his hell. So I just lived each day as it was given to me, whether right or wrong. I didn't know if I was coming or going.

Looking back

As a young adult........

Everything that I thought was good for me was just that for the moment.

Regardless of the certain situations I dealt with, it wasn't anything I couldn't really deal with or handle. This is what I thought to be my fun years.

Nothing, I felt, could stop me. I knew it all. I was sitting on top of the world.

No one had control of me, but me. I enjoyed being the center of attention.

Now I wasn't a part of the circle, I was the circle. I was in charge of you getting in or either getting out.

What I know now.......

The devil set me up!!!

For someone who thought they were so in control of their life, I easily provided the bear minimum for myself. I was the perfect candidate for the devil to take control and use me. I realized that if I was important enough for the devil to use me, I'm just as important for God to use me. For God is in control.

Chapter Seven

One Cold December Morning

Just when I thought things were going well, I received a page from daddy. I would hear from dad occasionally, or when I needed him, so this was not out of the ordinary. With no emotion, that I could tell, he said "Your mother is in the hospital, and they said she is brain dead, and she will not make it through the night." Of what was left of it, my heart broke! I immediately called Lisa to find out where mommy was and what really happened. Lisa said mommy is still able to recognize everyone, but she can't speak and she will move her thumb, if she understood you. We can't keep her on life support, for she will be brain dead for the rest of her life. What do you want to do?

"I'm on my way! Don't do anything, until I get there." I was to catch the plane out the next day. No sleep that night, I prayed like I never prayed before. Morning came, I called my dad, and my aunt picked up the phone. When she heard my voice, softly she whispered, "Your mom has died!" At a Jersey City payphone, I fell to the ground in sorrow.

I went to my grandmothers house immediately, and I called Lisa from there. She informed me that grandma, my mothers mother, took her off of life support. "Did no one understand me?" "I said to not do anything, until I got there." I became angry. Why wasn't I granted the

Journey To My Deliverance

opportunity to say mom I love you, and have her acknowledge that she understood that. Until present, no one had an answer. My father suggested that I not take the flight and leave the following day, since the body wasn't being transferred from VA., until then. I agreed. The entire trip down there was dreadful. All I could anticipate was seeing my mother. I talked to a star that night, the brightest one in the sky. It was a conversation I'd never had intimately before. It's a conversation that NO ONE needs to know. Hours later, we arrived in NC. I don't know exactly where we stopped first. I do know the next stop was the funeral home. Mommy's body wasn't ready yet, so I had to take care of the business matters, in which my mother's mother, had an input in everything. I felt since she made the decision for her to no longer exist, why not? They asked us to come back later that afternoon to view the body and make sure it was okay for viewing that evening.

Yea, this was quick. Christmas was just over, and people were getting ready for the new year.

We left the funeral parlor and went to clean out mommy's house. It wasn't really much to save. Some antique things that I still cherish to this day, some pictures that I made sure to keep.

Everything else was pretty much left or thrown away. As we were getting ready to leave and everyone was standing outside, I went back inside the house. It seems as if mommy knew I wanted her to know that I love her, but it was more important of what she had to say to me. I went into her room, and I sat on her bed. Next to her bed, on a night stand, there under a cup, laid two pieces of paper that had lost it's coloration from sitting out too long. I unfolded the letter and opened the water stained papers. It was dated May 28, 1995, seven months before her death. I began to read the letter which read:

Hi Son,

How is my wonderful son today and how have you been. I have talked to your father and he tells me some great things that you have achieved. I must tell you son, I am so proud of you more than you'll ever realize. Strive for the stars my son and always keep God in your heart soul. He can take you anywhere you wish to go. I miss you so much, Chris. Sometimes I think about you and the tears just burst through. Sometimes the pain is more than I can stand., because I miss my baby. The tears are following from my eyes as I write this letter to you. (That's when I realized the water stained paper was not from the cup that sat on the table.) *I want to hold you in my arms and tell you how much I love you and how I miss you. I wish that one day we can just sit down one day and talk and be mother and son. My health, especially my eyesight is failing me gradually. I feel death is coming to visit me soon.*

The letter closed by saying,

Well, son take care of yourself and continue to bring the house down with your performances. So take care of yourself and I hope to see you soon. I have so much to say to you, but I don't have that much paper, (smile). I love you, I love you, I love you. I cant's say or express it enough. Keep up the good work and may God continue to bless you, my son. Always know and feel my love and I wish only the best for everything for you my darling. God speed.

Love,
Mama
(Rosie)

Again, I shed no tear. We were on our way back to the funeral home, and the body was to be checked for viewing. I couldn't move as everyone else walked into the viewing room. "Come on, Chris", dad replied. My steps were short. As I entered the room, I could here the music so clearly, Precious Lord, Take my hand. There mom laid in the peach colored dress, in the charcoal coffin. I stood with no emotion, but then tears dripped from my weary eyes. It was a cry, that I had not cried before. I kissed the cheek of her rested body. I left.

I went to meet some of my friends (one now deceased), who came down to NC. I decided to stay with them at the hotel, until it was time to go to the wake. There was nothing special about the wake.

But there was one lady who I never seen a day in my life, that fell to her knees in tears, and when she arose, she placed a white rose on her chest. The lady then said, you were the only friend I had. The lady looked at me without a clue that I was the son of her only friend. The night ended. It was December 31st, the day of the funeral. There were cars that trail to the church for at least a mile. My cousin sang the song, I've learned to live Holy. Now it was my turn to give my mother something she never had the true essence of hearing. I sang "Eternal life" combined with "soon I will be done with the troubles of the world".

After the funeral was over we stopped at the repast, and I informed the fellows, that I wanted to be back in NJ before 12 midnight.

Looking Back

as a young adult and what I know now......

I started living a double life. I was saved one day, and sinning the next. I fell back into my own doings. I knew what was right and what was wrong, but I was allowing my decisions to create my future. I knew I had to make changes in my life. Mom wasn't there anymore. I felt a sense of really being out in the world alone.

Luke 16:13

No servant can serve two masters; for either he will hate the one and love the other, or he will be devoted to the one and despise the other. You cannot serve God and mammon."

Chapter Eight

A change is gonna come

We were back in New Jersey and I was home at 11:58pm.
Perfect timing to leave a few things behind, and move forward. This was a wake up call for me. Over and over I kept reading my mother's letter. What stuck out most is when she said 'Take care of yourself",
"Keep God In your Heart", and "I love you , I love you, I love you." All these things were necessary in my change that's gonna come. I began to re-direct my life. I started going to church every Sunday. I became more active in the choir. I even joined the Aids/ Awareness Task Force. I hadn't worked in years, and I landed a dietary job. I began working non-stop, and still going to church. I started to feel good about myself. What became hard for me was trying to get out of a situation I found myself locked into. But getting out led me to some of the same people and situations. A year later, sis came to live with me. I was sort of happy, but sad at the same time. I was really concerned about my two nephews down there with my grandma and my mother not being around anymore to step in. However, everything works for the good. Within that year, I bought my first new car. I was so excited. God was blessing me because I allowed Him to use me for His glory. I started to feel confident about myself. Even though the wall was still up, I felt pieces of it crumbling.

Journey To My Deliverance

I finally got out of the relationships that were hindering me; I was finally "taking care of myself." Sis and I got an apartment together. She was working at the Veterans hospital, and I was working no longer in dietary, because I had received a promotion with the same company, in another department. Look what happens when you do God's will. I started to remove things from my life and I allowed Him to use me more. I'd often reflect on the day my auntie in VA,. introduced me God. I was now the nurse staff coordinator for a 200 bed nursing center. I've never done anything like that a day in my life, but God, Oh but God!

Even when things were at it's best, tragedy came my way again.

My best friend, Carlos (my hanging buddy), took ill and died. Carlos and I did everything together. I mean we were sneaky. Nothing we did was so serious that we would end up in jail, but Carlos' mother was always shaking her head when we would say we're going out of town and we had no job and no money. Carlos was really like my brother.

He was the quiet sneaky little brother and I was the outspoken bad older brother. With every good, I realized there is a bad. Sometimes God has to remove to make room for bigger and better. Nevertheless, I went through my moment of sorrow, but embracing mama's advice in her letter, I kept God first. I later transitioned to another job where the money was better. I then bought my second car. I was dating here and there, but some, not all, meant nothing of seriousness to me. I got to keep it real. However, more and more, I started to feel the wall coming down. I finally had my own place and my own car. This was great. I knew how I wanted to live, and I made every effort to live that way. Even though I didn't have the house on the lake, I made sure there were certain amenities that I needed to have. I started hanging with more people that were saved. There were some stragglers, but God was removing. One thing about God's way, it's totally painless when you do it his way. He can remove people and you want even bat an eye when there gone. My friends started to fellowship together. I started to know more about myself and what I was capable of being. I started getting in shape. Within one year, my body was really coming together. Hey, I accomplished something that I put my mind to.

So it is here that, I took a step back (just one) and looked over the years what had been major accomplishments for me. I had and was dedicated to my God, church, friends, job, and home.

Yet there was something missing. I wanted to share it with someone. I wanted someone to experience the joy I had inside. I went through my first lay-off, but I still had my joy. He gave me another job, and I still had my joy. I was so desperate to share it. I began to fall in the trap of wanting to share it with the first person that said, "You look good." This was the one for me. All you had to tell me was my body was tight and face was sexy, and I was all yours. After three or four, "You look great", I'd had enough. I felt myself in similar situations as before. Still treating people anyway I felt, and making them feel less, so I could feel more. Somehow it just seemed to be working to my advantage. I never understood why people stayed around for as long as they did. Who wants to be treated any kind of way? I always felt that is was my great sex that was always bragged about among the crowds/circle, that kept them. Later, I found out that some were seeing the possibilities of someone to be great, if he just gets his act together.

I decided to take a vacation. I went to Punta Cano, DR. I decided when I got back, I'm going to do things differently. Then, I said you know what, I don't really want to be with anyone. As long as I have friends, I was okay. What brings me to this point is what made me write my story. I later fell in love with someone, who came and changed my life completely. I choose to leave them nameless, due to my protection and continuing love for them. Those who know me will make assumptions of who they think it may be, I'm almost certain they would probably be wrong. The mystery in me compels me to keep this one to myself. However, our time spent was wonderful. I mean dinners were great, the arguments made me love more. I was taken by total surprise. Not knowing at the time I still had traits that I never dealt with. Because of this, my traits invaded my relationship.

Insecurity took over. I became afraid. My traits got the best of me. I lost my job, I had no money, and friends were no where to be found. I felt abandoned from everyone and everything. I felt sorry for myself and that I wasn't worthy of anything. Ignoring the voice of God calling, I became selfish and had to answer God later. I had to fix the mess that I felt He put me in. How foolish for me to forget that Gods' way is painless and not let Him work it out. Well on top of that I felt I needed to have someone love me, but couldn't find anyone. How I messed up so badly. Why did I not break the generational curse? I cried for days. I held the knife in one hand and the Bible in the other.

Sunday came, and oh when Sunday comes. I got up with reservations on ever going back to church. At 10:30 I went anyway. I tried to refrain from crying. I put on the facade, that I was so accustomed to: smiling on the outside and falling apart on the inside.

From the moment I hit the choir stand. I just said, "LORD, I SURRENDER" and I fell to pieces. Not knowing it then, God was preparing to break me so that he can rebuild me. I had prayer warriors in every corner and I still didn't know what God wanted me to do. Later after church, I came home and I sat in the living room with no tv, but gospel music playing lightly in the background. I prayed to God and asked Him to show me what I needed to do in order to be what He needed me to be later. God would not answer. I cried, "God please, let me know and I will do it for you!" God didn't answer. Why did I again feel abandoned? Donnessa Victor, a Steward of Saint Matthew and a GREAT friend, sent a text message to me, asking if I was okay. Like a baby I wrote, "Why won't God answer me?" She told me to read Acts the 9th chapter. What stuck out most for me was the fourth to the twentieth verses.

Acts 9:4-20

[4] And he fell to the ground and heard a voice saying to him, "Saul, Saul, why do you persecute me?" 5 And he said, "Who are you, Lord?" And he said, "I am Jesus, whom you are persecuting; [6] but rise and enter the city, and you will be told what you are to do." [7] The men who were traveling with him stood speechless, hearing the voice but seeing no one. [8] Saul arose from the ground; and when his eyes were opened, he could see nothing; so they led him by the hand and brought him into Damascus. [9] And for three days he was

without sight, and neither ate nor drank. [10] Now there was a disciple at Damascus named Anani'as. The Lord said to him in a vision, "Anani'as." And he said, "Here I am, Lord." [11] And the Lord said to him, "Rise and go to the street called Straight, and inquire in the house of Judas for a man of Tarsus named Saul; for behold, he is praying, [12] and he has seen a man named Anani'as come in and lay his hands on him so that he might regain his sight." [13] But Anani'as answered, "Lord, I have heard from many about this man, how much evil he has done to thy saints at Jerusalem; [14] and here he has authority from the chief priests to bind all who call upon thy name." [15]

But the Lord said to him, "Go, for he is a chosen instrument of mine to carry my name before the Gentiles and kings and the sons of Israel; [16] for I will show him how much he must suffer for the sake of my name." [17] So Anani'as departed and entered the house. And laying his hands on him he said, Brother Saul, the Lord Jesus who appeared to you on the road by which you came, "has sent me that you may regain your sight and be filled with the Holy Spirit." [18] And immediately something like scales fell from his eyes and he regained his sight. Then he rose and was baptized, [19] and took food and was strengthened. For several days he was with the disciples at Damascus. [20] And in the synagogues immediately he proclaimed Jesus, saying, "He is the Son of God."

Basically what it revealed to me is that before Saul was made a saint, he was made to see himself as a great sinner. He was made to see the evil in himself that he never saw before. I realized that a humbling conviction of sin, is the first step toward saving a conversion of sin. God reminded me, remember when you looked back over your greatest accomplishment and you cried, "It was God, oh God"!

Yet you still sinned. Your sin was your ignorance and your foolishness, for I have given you the talent and the knowledge to have all things. Your ignorance caused you to sin against me. I never did anything to you. It was I who came from my heaven to do you good. It was I who died on the cross for you, and now you want to crucify me again? Why do you do the things that are not of me? How will you give reason for it? Go and find why you did what you did and then you will know the discernment of what unreasonable sin is.

So I went back over my life, and **I found the reasons** for my sins. I repented to my God, and began a stronger prayer life. I studied the scriptures more. I still see a professional counselor. All that was not of God was being removed. Daily I began to check myself. I asked God first and I sat still until I heard his voice. My thoughts weren't being clouded. Burdens had been lifted. Blessings, just of a new day, received more Praised; as Sin fled from my body, mind and soul. I became the parent of my actions, and I nurtured them everyday.

Before I could talk to anyone, or work at any job or go to any gym, I had to work on me. Out of the "looking back" I did, one thing stuck in my mind: I remembered an old church saying, "God will always bring you back." Remember when I first had the conversation with my aunt in Va., about wanting to know who this man, that made her life joyful?

There's a part in there where I remembered that one day God wants me to come and live with him, where his heaven is 100 times better than living on earth. That conversation is really what made me see one of the most important purposes for our lives today. We have to live according to the will of God, or we will live in a hell, that's 100 times worst than what we choose to live on earth. Right then and there, I had made my decision. I am leaving my hell, to get to His heaven!!!

Chapter Nine

I Know It Took A Miracle

Weeks had passed and I was moving in the right direction. My cell phone would ring like crazy, but I wouldn't answer. I went through a phase of working on who I needed to be and how I needed to minister to those around me. I then began to answer calls and inform those people about my change and what God is doing for me.

It's funny how you can mentioned change and God, and don't have to say anything else for people to remove themselves from your life.

Praise the Lord!!! My cell phone bill had never been so low.

I was still struggling with not having a job, no money, and eating every other day. Thanks to Chad and Jamal for the times they didn't take my foolish pride of me saying, "I'm okay". They would either bring me food or money to get something to eat. Davey, Keith, along with Rob (someone who God perfectly placed in my life) made sure I was also well taken care of. From Davey's humorous personality that made me strong, lil' Keith's (being Keith) would put me in my place about secluding myself from those who care about me, Robs anointed words of encouragement and of course to Donna who just told me like it really was, played an important role of rebuilding the good that I never let outshine the bad. Even to this day, Donna was one I went and cried my many tears. It seems as if I wasn't crying, she was.

Again weeks had passed and I received a job offer. The money wasn't bad and I needed to get hurriedly back into the work force.

Unemployment was quickly running out. However, shortly after I landed the job, I took very ill and had to go directly in the hospital. I developed an infection, which caused severe pain and bleeding. If I hadn't gone to the hospital any sooner, my sun would have set. I experienced the most excruciating pains I ever dealt with in my life.

Dad came to visit me, along with others, but I was so heavily drugged, I can't recall much of any conversations. I do remember dad's. How saddened he looked, and it seemed that he tried everything he could do to refrain from crying. I was fine with him not crying, if he was or wasn't. I was most happy with him just being there. That's all I really ever wanted from daddy, to just be there. Once he left, he never checked on me again, until weeks after I left the hospital. I didn't know if he could deal, or, well if he just couldn't deal. At any rate, life had to go on. I was happy that he invited me to several summer cook-outs.

If that was his way of showing his love, that was good enough for me.

We were spending time.

Still not fully recovered, I had to find work. My unemployment had stopped and I had no way of paying my rent. And yet, I didn't feel discouraged. I had interviews lined up and prayed on the possibilities of what could become. Earlier in the year, I had paid for a trip to Boca Chica (DR). There was no way of a refund, so I had no choice but to go. Along with Davey, we ventured to the island to regroup ourselves and come back to the States for a fresh start. During our stay, I had my morning devotions. The first morning I was lead to the book of Psalms the 118th chapter and the 17th and 18th verses. It stated **" I shall not die, but I shall live, and recount the deeds of the Lord. The Lord has chastened me sorely, but he has not given over to death."** I began to rejoice. I knew that God had spared me and was not going to take away my life, for I had to declare all that he has done for me. Praise Ye The Lord!!!

Time for us to depart and head back to the world where we truly belonged. I had an interview lined up that Monday following our Saturday return. Unfortunately, the interviewer misread my resume and was looking for a different candidate. But look how God works.

The interviewer said, there's a place where he went to get work and was sent to the present company for which I interviewed. Even though I was a bit discouraged, he gave me an old business card of an agency that had a name of someone who I later found out, didn't work there any longer. Again, I became a bit discouraged. When I called the company from downstairs, I asked for the name of the person on the card. After discussing with her who I was and how I was referred, she became baffled and asked me who I was looking for. I gave her the entire name on the card, and she stated I had the wrong person.

She proceeded to ask me what exactly was I looking for and I informed her of what I wanted to do. She asked me when was I able to come in and meet with her. As it turns out, this lady was the director in the field of nurse recruitment. I thought I was going to meet with her, in order for her to find me an outside job, but she and her boss interviewed me that day for an internal position. They asked me to come back later that week to discuss opportunities within their company. The next day, I received a phone call and email regarding a position I had applied for months ago. This young lady stated they were interested in me joining their company, but would like to go through one more interview. On top of that I received two more calls from medical recruitment firms. This is evident of how much better God is to me, than I was to myself. By this time I was one month behind in my rent and was being called by the rental office everyday regarding when I would be able to pay my rent. Suddenly, I realized that my faith was pretty much all I had to offer. With no real guarantee of a job, I went to the rental office and informed them that in three weeks, I will pay them $500 a week until I am caught up on my rent.

They agreed. Still with no call backs from any interviewers, a week had passed, but my faith was all I had, and that was more than good enough for me. I knew that God was in the process of working

Journey To My Deliverance

something out. I just didn't know exactly when, but I felt it coming soon. I prayed without ceasing and I cut myself off from the world.

It was just me and God. I went to church that Sunday. I worshiped and praised God as if the miracle He had worked, was already done. I went home that evening, watched television, listened to music, and went to bed. Monday morning, I got up, had my prayer/devotion, and ate my cheerios. While watching the ending of Live w/ Regis and Kelly, my phone rung. On the other end was the vibrant voice of a young lady who asked me if I was still interested in the nurse recruiter position. Eagerly, I said yes. She asked me when could I start, I stated, "I would like to start tomorrow". She replied, "We would like for you to start tomorrow". We hung up the phone and let's just say, my praise break is still going on. I took an offer in the city of New York, where I'm currently employed. I thank God everyday for stepping in on time. It is so true when you hear the testimonies of the saints, "He may not come when you want Him, but He's always on time". I had a relapse and had to go back into the hospital about one month after I started my position. I didn't worry about losing my job, because God had proven himself over and over again. So I had no doubt that he would bring me out. My manager called me twice in the week that I was out, expressing her concern about how I was doing.

Towards the end of that week, one of the other managers called to see if I would return to work on the following Monday. "Yes, I will." I am still employed with the company that resides in New York City. No major complications have happened physically, since then. Everyday I look to the hills from where my help cometh. Even though some days seem more painful than others, everyday gets better for me.

God will still remain the start and the finish of it all. Even though I'm faced with discomfort, sometimes daily, I see my pain as God cleaning me out. Because I had so much junk inside, it is going to hurt until God cleanses me thoroughly. I have chosen to put God first. He orders me on how I need to live and treat people. He sets my mind at ease. He assures me everyday, by waking me up, that he has me in is every care. I don't worry about the world or what it has to say or offer me. I have a Jesus! I don't worry about getting involved or lost in the crowd. I have Jesus! I don't need to find love. I have Jesus!

Friends may come and friends may go. I have Jesus! For what ever God has for me, it is for me. So I'll just wait on the Lord. God is the supplier of everything, even before my creation.

During the course of looking back and writing out my life, I have been able to deal with myself. Since then, I have been getting stronger. It is my prayer that my light will not shine only in church, but to everyone, I have wronged, mislead, and deceived. I pray that my light will shine to everyone and everywhere I go. Life has new meaning, and it is not my plan, but it is my duty to live it more abundantly. Let me be truly honest, I still may not be all God needs me to be, but God is not through with me yet. For we ALL have sinned and come short of His glory. Everyday I am faced with stronger temptations, but I realize no temptation is worth me reaping again, what I had sown. God is the light for the road that I must follow.

We often here people say, " I could have been dead buried in my grave". Well I truly know what they mean. For when I look back over MY LIFE, one thing truly comes to mind: I know it took a miracle!!! Everyday I face the hell I lived in. I choose to face it, in order to deal with it and move on to the greater prosperities for my life. It took God to break me, in order to rebuild me. He is cleaning the impurities from the inside to the outside and everyday, I'm thankful.

How do I know that the inside and the outside are being cleaned? I feel God's power working everyday. My life was once filled with gaining the things of this world. That no longer matters to me.

Although I still reside, for the past five years in the same complex, the beautiful apartment I once had (fully furnished), no longer exists. A television, a couch, and a table is pretty much all that remains for now. The 170lbs of solid muscle, I worked so hard to get is also gone.

However, I'm more than thankful for what I have right now; more than I've ever had in my life. There's a song that the Inspirational choir of Saint Matthew sings which is a true testament for my life. "Gain the world, but give me Jesus." Everyday I want to wake up and taste and see that the Lord is still good. I am adamant when it comes to listening to everyone else, for I here the voice of Jesus, telling me to still fight on. For He promised never to leave me, never to leave me alone. I'm not persuaded by comments on whether I look good to you or not. We are all just dust from which we came, and it will be the same dust from which we will return. So as I conclude portions of my life, I pray that you will take certain steps in regaining the life the devil is trying to steal. Ask yourself, what does this world really have to offer, that will last even after you're gone? What or who can you take with you?

Are you in need of your deliverance? Do you want it bad enough?

Out of all the goals we have set, set your daily goal as taking control by giving God complete control. My life has and is changing more everyday. NO means NO and without explanation. Excuses have no entry. Fear has no future. Doubt is dead. Procrastination is not permitted. Greed is gone. Sin is not successful. Slothfulness has surrendered.

Find your faith, and let God, the author and finisher of it all, handle the rest. You will be amazed, just as I am. For I assure you, in this life there is a journey to deliverance.

Psalms 50:15

"And call upon me in the day of trouble: I will deliver thee, and thou shalt glorify me."

THE END

Printed in the United States
45880LVS00005B/154-162